Monitoring the Progress of
SHIPBUILDING
PROGRAMMES

How Can the Defence Procurement Agency
More Accurately Monitor Progress?

Mark V. Arena • John Birkler • John F. Schank
Jessie Riposo • Clifford A. Grammich

Prepared for the United Kingdom's Ministry of Defence
Approved for public release; distribution unlimited

EUROPE

The research described in this report was sponsored by the United Kingdom's Ministry of Defence. The research was conducted jointly in RAND Europe and the RAND National Security Research Division.

Library of Congress Cataloging-in-Publication Data

Monitoring the progress of shipbuilding programmes : how can the Defence Procurement Agency more accurately monitor progress? / Mark V. Arena ... [et al.].
    p. cm.
    "MG-235."
    Includes bibliographical references and index.
    ISBN 0-8330-3660-2 (pbk.)
    1. Great Britain. Royal Navy—Procurement. 2. Defence Procurement Agency (Great Britain)—Management. 3. Shipbuilding industry—Great Britain—Management. I. Arena, Mark V.

VC265.G7M66 2004
359.8'3'0681—dc22
                                                                    2004018825

The RAND Corporation is a nonprofit research organization providing objective analysis and effective solutions that address the challenges facing the public and private sectors around the world. RAND's publications do not necessarily reflect the opinions of its research clients and sponsors.

RAND® is a registered trademark.

Cover design by Stephen Bloodsworth

Published 2005 by the RAND Corporation
1776 Main Street, P.O. Box 2138, Santa Monica, CA 90407-2138
1200 South Hayes Street, Arlington, VA 22202-5050
201 North Craig Street, Suite 202, Pittsburgh, PA 15213-1516
RAND URL: http://www.rand.org/
To order RAND documents or to obtain additional information, contact
Distribution Services: Telephone: (310) 451-7002;
Fax: (310) 451-6915; Email: order@rand.org

Preface

The Defence Procurement Agency (DPA), part of the UK Ministry of Defence (MOD), measures its annual performance against five key targets for its top 20 projects (by value), as documented in its Major Project Reports. Key Target 2 addresses programme slippage, which is the delay between the promised in-service date and the actual or projected in-service date. The MOD 2001/2002 performance report indicates slippage for the top 20 projects averaged approximately one year. Furthermore, the existences of delays are recognised very late in the programme. Because the Major Project Reports cover all areas of DPA programmes, the programme slippage they indicate includes more than shipbuilding programmes. Nevertheless, recent delays for programmes such as the Landing Platform Dock, Astute, and Auxiliary Oiler indicate slippage does specifically occur in shipbuilding.

The issue of programme slippage and the inability to recognise delays early in the programme led the DPA to ask the RAND Corporation to

- assess how shipbuilders (and other industries) track programme progress and how they identify a set of metrics that are used to measure progress
- consider how the DPA should monitor programmes and recommend the types of information that shipbuilders should report to enable the agency to independently assess shipbuilding progress

- identify why ships are delivered late and understand why commercial shipbuilders have much better schedule performance.

This monograph is one of a set of three addressing related issues in UK shipbuilding. Funded by the DPA, the three studies have the common goal of contributing to understanding better the warship-building industry within the United Kingdom and to improving management processes therein. The other two monographs answer the following specific questions:

- How could greater use of advanced outfitting and of outsourcing reduce shipyard workload in the Future Aircraft Carrier programme and thus increase the likelihood of on-schedule completion of that and other DPA programmes? (MG-198-MOD)
- How do military and commercial shipbuilding differ, and what are the implications for diversifying the UK shipbuilding industry's customer base? (MG-236-MOD)

This report should be of special interest not only to the DPA but also to service and defence agency managers and policymakers involved in shipbuilding on both sides of the Atlantic. It should also be of interest to shipbuilding industrial executives in the United Kingdom.

This research was sponsored by the MOD and conducted within RAND Europe and the International Security and Defense Policy Center of the RAND National Security Research Division, which conducts research for the US Department of Defense, allied foreign governments, the intelligence community, and foundations.

For more information on RAND Europe, contact the president, Martin van der Mandele. He can be reached by email at mandele@ rand.org; by phone at +31 71 524 5151; or by mail at RAND Europe, Netonweg 1, 2333 CP Leiden, The Netherlands. For more information on the International Security and Defense Policy Center, contact the director, Jim Dobbins. He can be reached by email at James_Dobbins@rand.org; by phone at (310) 393-0411, extension

5134; or by mail at RAND Corporation, 1200 South Hayes Street, Arlington, VA 22202-5050 USA. More information about RAND is available at www.rand.org.

Contents

Figures

Tables

Summary

Introduction

The Defence Procurement Agency (DPA), part of the UK Ministry of Defence (MOD), provides services and equipment for the national security of the United Kingdom. This task requires efficient capital management. One of the keys to efficient capital expenditure is good programme management.

Cost and schedule control and estimating are central competencies of programme management. Controlling cost and schedule is the principal focus of this report. Continually updated knowledge of project status is important for both operational planning (determining when the customer will have use of the asset) and financial management (determining cash flow needed to support the programme). A good control system can also aid programme improvement by identifying problem areas before they greatly affect production. Accurate estimating of changing programme needs allows an organisation to make best use of limited funding. The importance of estimating and control has been recognised by the DPA in that two of the five key targets monitored are related to cost and schedule performance.

The DPA measures its annual performance against five key targets. Key Target 2 relates to programme slippage, i.e., the delay between the promised in-service date and the actual or projected in-service date. The MOD indicates average programme slippage results in product delivery approximately one year later than the date originally anticipated at Main Gate (MOD, 2002a). Moreover, for military shipbuilding, slippage is often recognised very late in the programme, making it more difficult to overcome. Although measures of slippage cover MOD programmes broadly, recent shipbuilding programmes such as the Landing Platform Dock, Astute, and Auxiliary Oiler have been documented as suffering slippage as well (Scott, 2004).

These issues led the DPA to ask the RAND Corporation to

- assess how shipbuilders (and other industries) track programme progress and how they identify a set of metrics that are used to measure progress
- consider how the DPA should monitor programmes and recommend the types of information that should be gathered from shipbuilders to help the agency to independently assess shipbuilding progress
- identify why ships are delivered late and understand why commercial shipbuilders have much better schedule performance.

Methodology

To address these issues, RAND researchers

- surveyed major shipbuilders in the United Kingdom, United States, and European Union[1] and conducted follow-up, in-depth interviews with representatives of these firms; from these surveys and discussions, we identified which metrics are most commonly used to track shipbuilding progress

---

[1] For simplicity, throughout this report, the authors use the term 'European Union', or 'EU', to refer to those non-UK European shipbuilders surveyed (even though the United Kingdom is an EU member). Specifically, EU countries that participated consist of Finland, France, Italy, the Netherlands, and Spain (see Table 1.1 for the full list of shipbuilders).

- asked, for comparison purposes, representatives of the project management department of a major oil firm about their methods for tracking project progress
- reviewed literature on these major metrics to assess the advantages and disadvantages of each
- identified the primary causes of production delays for shipbuilders.

How Shipbuilders Monitor Progress

We classify the methods identified to track schedule progress metrics into six general categories: earned value related, milestones, task oriented, actual versus planned, area/zone (such as compartment completion), and other (a residual category). We asked the shipbuilders to report their primary schedule control metric during each of the six phases of shipbuilding: design, module block construction, assembly, outfitting, testing/trials, and commissioning.

Figure S.1 shows the proportion of shipbuilders using a particular metric at each phase of construction. Earned value management (EVM) metrics are the most commonly used in each phase of production, though less frequently in later phases; milestones are the second most commonly used.

US shipyards are more likely than UK or EU shipyards to use EVM throughout production, largely because of the US Department of Defense requirements for EVM on most acquisition programmes. UK and EU shipyards are more likely to use non-EVM metrics such as compartment completion (area/zone) and milestones, particularly towards the end of production.

Figure S.1
Shipbuilder Use of Metrics at Various Production Phases

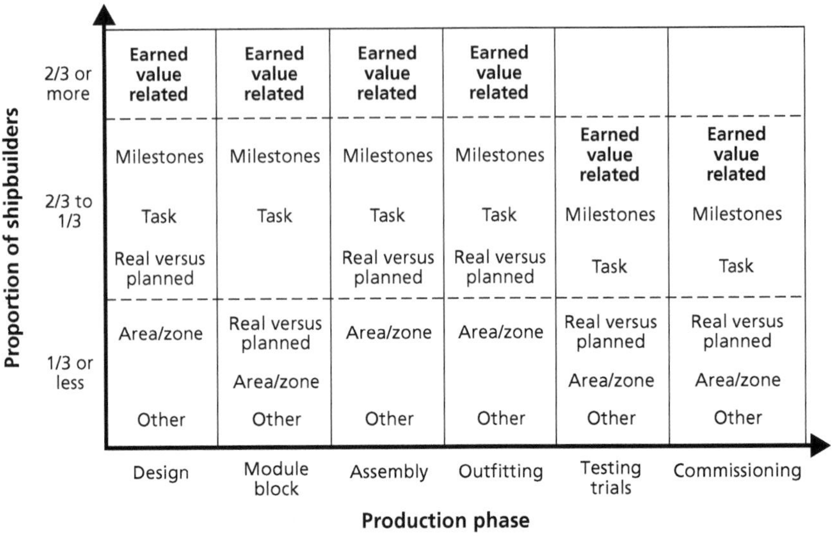

Proportion of shipbuilders	Design	Module block	Assembly	Outfitting	Testing trials	Commissioning
2/3 or more	Earned value related	Earned value related	Earned value related	Earned value related		
2/3 to 1/3	Milestones	Milestones	Milestones	Milestones	Earned value related	Earned value related
	Task	Task	Task	Task	Milestones	Milestones
	Real versus planned		Real versus planned	Real versus planned	Task	Task
1/3 or less	Area/zone	Real versus planned	Area/zone	Area/zone	Real versus planned	Real versus planned
		Area/zone			Area/zone	Area/zone
	Other	Other	Other	Other	Other	Other

Production phase

RAND *MG235-S.1*

What Progress Information Should the DPA Require of Shipbuilders?

The DPA should request from shipbuilders the basic information needed for EVM. The core measures are

- actual cost of work performed
- budget cost of work performed
- budget cost of work scheduled
- estimate at completion
- budget at completion.

From these measures, most of the derived EVM metrics can be calculated. These data should be readily available, since most UK shipyards already track production progress with an EVM system. Beyond the total programme level, these data should be reported at a lower level of detail (i.e., by work breakdown structure, major activity, and trade levels) and collected both cumulatively and by time period.

Because EVM does not account for how activities should be placed in sequence or what their effects are for critical paths, additional schedule control information should be tracked. The DPA should ask shipbuilders to provide updated, forecasted completion dates for each progress report. These reports should present revised critical path analyses for high-level activities on the network schedule. The agency should also track programme-specific milestones for each ship. Finally, the DPA should monitor the value of unresolved (unadjudicated) changes, which can help determine whether the amount of potential new work could cause the schedule to slip.

Developing Realistic Schedule Expectations

Being able to track progress is but one part of the problem the DPA faces in better schedule adherence. Other keys to solving this problem include the schedules the DPA itself sets for production and understanding elements of commercial shipbuilding that ensure on-time delivery that could be adapted to military construction.

The DPA typically sets initial in-service dates based on operational needs. The production schedule required to meet these dates may not be realistic or result in the most cost-effective procurement. The DPA should consider developing schedule norms similar to those used by other industries and based on prior programme performance to determine whether its production schedules are realistic.

Adapting Commercial Practices

Commercial shipbuilding has very different schedule performance than does the DPA or other military programmes. When asked about schedule performance, the common response from the commercial firms was: 'We are never late'. (Of course, such performance is only that reported by the firms we interviewed, not that for all commercial firms.) The reasons for their better, on-time performance include differences in commercial and military needs, in how each sector manages change, and in incentives of commercial contracts.

Change Orders and Late Product Definition: Major Contributors to Schedule Slips

We asked each shipbuilder to identify the factors that contribute to schedule slippage. The most frequently identified category was change orders/late product definition, cited nearly half the time (see Figure S.2). The second most cited reason for schedule slippage was the lack of timely technical information needed from a supplier or client.

Figure S.2
Causes of Schedule Slips Reported by Shipbuilders (percentage)

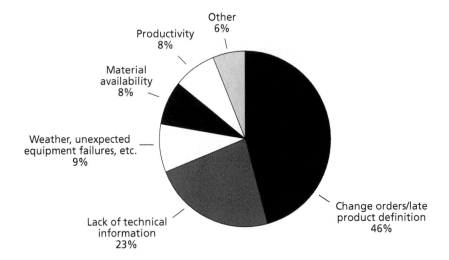

Perhaps more significant is the total amount of change that typically occurs in a programme. The average value of change on commercial contracts is 4 percent of the total contract cost; for military contracts, it is 8 percent. Furthermore, changes on military contracts take much longer to resolve, from four to 22 weeks, compared with one to five weeks for commercial contracts. Changes on military contracts also occur much later in the production phase than do those for commercial contracts. Shipyard representatives reported that more than half the change in commercial contracts occurs during the design phase. About 40 percent of military contract changes occur during design, with more taking place in the later phases of production, particularly in assembly and outfitting.

Commercial Incentives Heavily Weighted Towards On-Time Delivery
Commercial shipbuilding contracts include more incentives for on-time delivery. The contracts may impose significant liquidated damages for late delivery, costing thousands of pounds per day. To avoid such penalties, commercial shipbuilders are willing to spend money on outsourcing to get the project back on track. The full order books for many commercial contractors provide a further incentive for on-time delivery; if one programme is delayed, other programmes will also slip. Because most commercial contracts are for fixed prices, commercial shipbuilders want to move production through a facility as quickly as possible to maximise profit. The DPA has used liquidated damage clauses on recent shipbuilding contracts (e.g., for the Astute and Type 45 programmes), but whether such clauses serve as schedule incentives is debatable.

The structure of commercial contracts also provides an incentive for on-time delivery. Typically, 80 percent of the contract value is paid on delivery. The shipyard carries the financial burden on the ship (i.e., interest on the loan needed for its construction) until delivery. In contrast, military contracts are typically paid using progress milestones that are intended to keep the shipbuilder in a cash-neutral position. Some of the initiatives under Smart Acquisition (the MOD's acquisition process), such as the Public Finance Initiative, are moving procurement strategies to more commercial terms and incentives. Still, the practicality for such an approach for a warship is unclear.

Conclusions and Recommendations

Nearly all shipbuilders use EVM as a method to monitor the progress of design and production. The method is well established in many areas of business (commercial and military), not just shipbuilding. As a result, there are extensive training, software, consulting, and literature resources for implementing it. Because UK shipbuilders already use this methodology as part of their internal control process, the DPA would not, in applying it for the agency's own purposes, be asking the shipbuilders to develop or implement new systems. The effective use of EVM will require the DPA to staff Integrated Project Teams (IPTs) with EVM professionals. The DPA has the opportunity to improve its change management on shipbuilding programmes, which could benefit both cost and schedule performance.

In sum, the DPA should consider the following actions to improve the schedule performance of its shipbuilding programmes:

- Develop an internal set of schedule norms to set realistic expectations.
- Consider options to control or reduce changes, especially those late in the process.
- Resolve changes quickly.
- Require shipbuilders to report EVM data that the shipyards already track for internal purposes.
- Make the EVM process a management control function of the IPT.
- Require shipbuilders to report estimated delivery date and critical path analysis.
- Set appropriate incentives on ship contracts to encourage better schedule performance.

Acknowledgements

This report would not have been possible without the contributions of several firms and individuals. First, we would like to thank Andy McClelland of the DPA for guiding this research and providing contacts within the MOD. We also would like to thank Muir Mac-Donald (Astute program) and Keith Prentice (Type 45 program), the IPT team leaders who sponsored this research. We would like to thank Philip Koenig (Office of Naval Research) and Harry Thie (RAND) for their review of the report and the many improvements and suggestions they made. Professor Thomas Lamb (University of Michigan) participated in the study's data collection and made several helpful suggestions for the analysis—we thank him for his time and help. Finally, we are deeply indebted to the shipbuilders that participated in the study survey and interviews. Without their assistance, this research would not have been possible.

Abbreviations

ACWP	actual cost of work performed
BAC	budget at completion
BCWP	budgeted cost of work performed
BCWS	budgeted cost of work scheduled
CEV	customer earned value
CPI	cost performance index
CV	cost variance
DoD	Department of Defense (US)
DPA	Defence Procurement Agency
EAC	estimate at completion
ETC	estimate to complete
EVM	earned value management
IPT	Integrated Project Team
NAO	National Audit Office
SPI	schedule performance index
SV	schedule variance
TCPI	to-complete cost performance index
WBS	work breakdown structure

CHAPTER ONE

Introduction

The Defence Procurement Agency (DPA), part of the UK Ministry of Defence (MOD), provides services and equipment necessary for the security of the United Kingdom. Although the agency does not generate a positive cash flow, as does a private venture, it still must make efficient and effective use of its capital. Defence procurement is expensive, and DPA expenditures, like those for any organisation, are constrained by available funding. Only so many financial resources can be spent on defence, since there are many competing funding issues the government faces. The DPA must not only be selective in the programmes it funds but also procure items efficiently. Efficient capital expenditure requires good programme management.

Accurate estimating and cost and schedule control are central competencies of programme management. Accurate estimating allows an organisation to make the best use of limited funding. Consistently underestimating cost or schedule needs can lead to cash flow problems and possible programme cancellations. Overestimating these needs reduces capital available for additional programmes. The DPA has recognised the importance of estimating and control by focusing two of its five key targets on cost and schedule performance. Controlling cost and schedule is the principal focus of this report. Monitoring cost and schedule is important for both operational planning (determining the product delivery date) and financial management (determining the cash flow needed to support the programme). A good control system can also aid programme improvement by helping identify problem areas.

This report focuses on schedule and progress metrics while recognising there is some overlap with cost control metrics. In practice, these issues are intertwined and cannot be easily isolated from one another.

Major UK Defence Acquisitions Are Typically Behind Schedule

The DPA gauges its annual performance against five key targets for its top 20 projects, which are measured by value and documented in the agency's Major Project Reports. Key Target 2 addresses programme slippage, the delay between the promised dates and actual or projected in-service dates. The MOD indicates that average slippage for its top 20 projects is approximately one year (United Kingdom Ministry of Defence, 2002a) beyond the delivery date approved at Main Gate. Because the Major Project Reports cover all areas of DPA programmes, the indicated slippage includes more than just shipbuilding programmes, the focus of this report. Nevertheless, recent delays for programmes such as the Landing Platform Dock, Astute, and Auxiliary Oiler indicate that slippage does occur in shipbuilding. Average in-year slippage for these major projects, i.e., that occurring within the annual reporting period, was 1.1 months, compared with a target of 0.4 months (MOD, 2003).

DPA Often Does Not Realise Projects Are Behind Schedule Until Late in the Production Cycle

Some slippage shows up early, but the bulk of it is often not recognised until the latter stages of the procurement cycle (NAO, 2002). Overall, schedule (or time) variance occurs very early, levels off midway through the procurement cycle, and increases again late in the cycle (see Figure 1.1). Cost variance, conversely, does not occur early, increases at the greatest rate midway through the procurement cycle, and levels off late in the cycle.

There are many possible explanations for these patterns. The early increase in schedule variance could be due to optimism being supplanted by better project definition and more realistic expectations, or after the project is approved and the contractor faces less pressure to 'look good'. The later schedule variance may be a result of technical and integration issues that typically do not surface until the end of the procurement cycle. In addition, changes or growth in cost may be easier to quantify than those for scheduling and thus are recognised earlier.[1]

Figure 1.1
Procurement Life Cycle Cost Variation Versus Time Variation

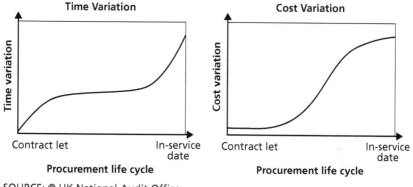

SOURCE: © UK National Audit Office.
RAND *MG235-1.1*

---

[1] One of the reviewers offered an additional explanation:

> With poor accuracy control . . . various stages of production can be churning out 'on time' (but dimensionally varying) intermediate products. Every process is indeed meeting its schedule, and everyone is happy. Then when it comes to final assembly (late in the programme), all of a sudden things just don't fit together and all sorts of time-consuming, handcrafted rework must be done. There goes the schedule.

Commercial Ships Are Typically Produced On Time

Commercial shipbuilding has much better schedule performance (see Figure 1.2). Asked about schedule performance, representatives of commercial firms regularly told us, 'We are never late'. In fact, one of the commercial shipbuilders we surveyed had only once delivered a ship after the contract delivery date since 1985. This less-than-one-month slippage was a result of damage during transport of a long lead item.

To be sure, there are substantial differences between commercial and military shipbuilding. For example, commercial ships are typically built from a well-established design, while military ships are more unique. Nevertheless, the management of change in particular, in both processes and in other industries, may offer some insights for those interested in reducing slippage.

Figure 1.2
Representative Commercial Shipbuilder's Delivery Performance, 1985–2001

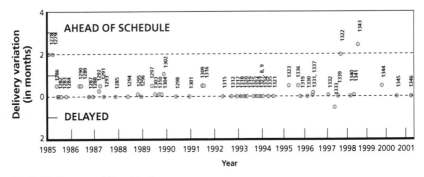

SOURCE: Kvaerner Masa-Yards.
NOTE: Deliveries according to contracted delivery time (all contracts).
RAND *MG235-1.2*

Areas of Inquiry

The issue of programme slippage and the inability to recognise delays early in the programme led the DPA to ask the RAND Corporation to

- assess how shipbuilders, and other industries, track programme progress and how they identify a set of metrics that are used to measure progress
- consider how the DPA should monitor programmes and recommend the types of information topics that should be gathered from shipbuilders to enable the agency to independently assess shipbuilding progress
- identify why ships are delivered late and understand why commercial shipbuilders have much better schedule performance.

Answering these questions requires a broad perspective, much more than a simple focus on metrics. Accordingly, we address other areas of management and production practice, particularly programme management. The ability to track progress ('progress reporting') and estimate schedules is important in identifying and correcting problems or shortfalls as programmes proceed. Being able to manage, limit, and efficiently handle change is important in keeping a programme on time and budget. The ability to forecast progress and schedule needs can be the most difficult aspect of keeping a project on schedule. Finally, incentives and payment strategies can align shipbuilder priorities with those of the DPA.

Realistic baseline expectations can also help avoid later slippage. Unrealistic expectations will cause programme slippage, regardless of the control methods employed, and can create a culture intolerant of critical or honest evaluation of progress. In such circumstances, being the messenger of 'bad news' could be career threatening. Furthermore, control becomes impossible when the baseline expectations are unrealistic.[2]

Knowing where you are with respect to budget and schedule is only part of the problem. More importantly, being able to forecast where you expect to be and how you will get there is another aspect of the often-difficult task of managing progress and schedule.

Methodology

We used a four-part methodology to address our areas of inquiry.

First, we surveyed major shipbuilders in the United Kingdom, United States, and European Union[3] (the survey form is reproduced in Appendix C). The survey included questions about such programme areas as schedule tracking methods, change control, causes of slippage, and forecasting.

Second, after receiving responses to these surveys, we had follow-on conversations with the shipbuilders to better understand the survey information, ensure that the forms had been completed in a consistent manner, and allow the shipbuilders to discuss relevant issues not captured in the survey. Most shipbuilders used this opportunity to show us a sample progress report. From those surveys and discussions, we determined metrics commonly used by shipbuilders. For comparison purposes, we also interviewed representatives from the project management department of a major oil firm in regards to their practices for cost and schedule control.

Third, we reviewed relevant literature to assess the advantages and disadvantages of the metrics we had identified. For example,

---

[2] Overoptimism is not just limited to the DPA. The recent National Audit Office report (*Ministry of Defence: Major Projects Report 2002*) indicating significant cost overruns in several pre–Smart Acquisition programs has raised questions about the soundness of contractors' bids on defence procurements. A *Times Online* article (PA News, 2004) suggests that contractors quote unrealistically low prices to win contracts.

[3] For simplicity, throughout this report, the authors use the term 'European Union', or 'EU', to refer to those non-UK European shipbuilders surveyed (even though the United Kingdom is an EU member). Specifically, EU countries that participated consist of Finland, France, Italy, the Netherlands, and Spain (see Table 1.1 for the full list of shipbuilders).

there are many studies that report on the US Department of Defense's (DoD's) experience with cost and schedule control.[4]

Fourth, we reviewed the primary causes of production delays identified by shipbuilders. Such information may help the DPA not only to monitor progress and anticipate potential delays but to avoid practices that contribute to schedule slippage.

The surveyed firms are a variety of shipbuilders in the United Kingdom, United States, and European Union (see Table 1.1). In the United Kingdom, all the major shipbuilders that produce and repair naval ships and submarines participated in the survey, as did Ferguson Shipbuilders, a producer of commercial and survey vessels. We also discussed schedule control practice with Appledore, a firm that did not formally complete a survey. In the United States, we surveyed most of the 'big six' naval shipbuilders, as well as Kvaerner Philadelphia, a commercial US shipbuilder. EU shipbuilders interviewed comprised cruise-ship builders that provided information on the schedule control methods they employ as well as shipbuilders constructing both commercial and military vessels.

Table 1.1
UK, US, and EU Shipbuilders Surveyed

UK Shipbuilders	US Shipbuilders	EU Shipbuilders
BAE Systems	Bath Iron Works	Chantiers de l'Atlantique (France)
Babcock BES-Rosyth	Electric Boat	
Devonport Management Ltd.	Kvaerner Philadelphia	Fincantieri (Italy)
	National Steel and Shipbuilding Company	IZAR (Spain)
Ferguson		Kvaerner Masa (Finland)
Swan Hunter	Northrop Grumman Ship Systems	Royal Schelde (The Netherlands)
Vosper Thornycroft		

---

[4] For example, see references and links provided on the Office of the Under Secretary of Defense (Acquisition, Technology & Logistics) Acquisition Resources & Analysis/Acquisition Management's Web site on EVM at www.acq.osd.mil/pm/.

Organisation of This Report

We present our findings in the four subsequent chapters, supplemented by three appendixes. Chapter Two summarises the survey results of how shipbuilders monitor design and production progress. Chapter Three documents information that the DPA should consider tracking to monitor progress. Chapter Four examines the causes of late ship delivery and how they vary for military and commercial shipbuilding. Chapter Five provides overall conclusions and recommendations.

Many of the metrics for monitoring progress are those of earned value management (EVM). Appendix A provides an overview of EVM for those who are unfamiliar with it; Appendix B provides a list of common EVM metrics; and Appendix C reproduces the survey we used to collect data from the shipbuilders.

CHAPTER TWO

How Do Shipbuilders Monitor Progress During Design and Production?

The metrics we identified to measure shipbuilding progress can be classified into six categories: earned value related, milestones, task oriented, actual versus planned, area/zone (such as compartment completion), and other (a residual category) (see Table 2.1).

Earned value–related metrics are those associated with EVM (see Appendix A). Earned value metrics compare the budgeted cost of work performed (BCWP) with the budgeted cost of work scheduled (BCWS) at a given point in time. Projects with a BCWP value less than that of the BCWS are considered behind schedule, while those with a BCWP value exceeding the BCWS value are considered ahead of schedule. Essentially, EVM weights cumulative task progress by estimated value.

Milestones are major events in the course of a programme. They range from very high-level events such as first block in dry dock, ship launch or float out, and system light off to those low-level events dealing with specific tasks. One shipbuilder, for example, tracks multiple milestones per structural unit.

Task-oriented metrics are based on the completing or starting of specific tasks or work packages. They are related to EVM methods but don't weight by task value.

Actual-versus-planned metrics are those tracking progress as a ratio of actual results to planned results. They differ from earned

Table 2.1
Schedule Metrics Categories

Earned valued related	• Actual cost of work performed • Budget cost of work scheduled • Budget cost of work performed • Cost performance index • Schedule performance index

Milestones	• Examples:
	  –start of construction
	  –delivery
	  –float out

Task oriented	• Percentage of tasks
	  –complete
	  –meeting start or completion date
	• Work packages

Actual versus planned	• Percentage of
	  –estimated cost spent
	  –estimated hours used
	  –weight installed

Area/zone	• Number of
	  –blocks installed
	  –compartments complete
	  –compartments accepted

Other	• Schedule/float contingency • Changes open • Other

value in that, while earned value measures progress relative to that planned, actual-versus-planned metrics focus more generally on actual accomplishments such as cumulative number of hours worked to date compared with estimated total hours needed to complete the job. These types of metrics can be more sensitive than EVM metrics to such issues as performance and estimating errors.

Area/zone, or compartment-completion, metrics focus on areas or zones of the ship. These metrics are generally used towards the end of production.

Other metrics are those we gathered that did not fit into the categories above. Examples of such metrics include available schedule float or contingency and amount of change unadjudicated.

Earned Value Metrics Dominate Primary Progress Measures

We asked the shipbuilders to identify the 'primary' progress metric they used during the various phases of production—that is, their main method of assessing progress. Figure 2.1 shows the amount of shipyards that reported using a metric from one of the six categories. We examined usage during six different phases: design, module block construction, assembly, outfitting, testing/trials, and commissioning. For each phase, we rank primary metrics by their reported prevalence of use and indicate the proportion of shipbuilders that report using them.

The reader should be aware of some qualifications in interpreting reported use of primary metrics. Some shipyards reported using more than one primary metric in a production phase. Not all shipyards reported metrics for all phases; repair shipyards, for example, do

Figure 2.1
Shipbuilder Use of Metrics at Various Production Phases

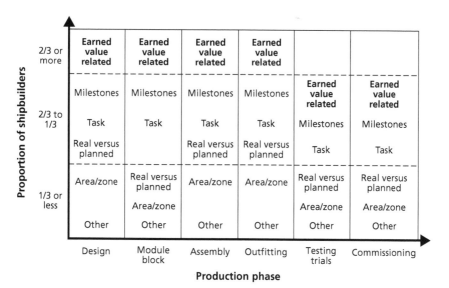

not have module block production or assembly activities and therefore did not report metrics for those phases.

Earned value metrics are the most commonly used in all production phases but are less frequently employed in the later phases. Milestone metrics are the second most commonly used.

Earned value metrics are particularly common in US shipyards. In fact, every US shipyard we surveyed uses earned value metrics as its primary metric for evaluating progress in every phase of production (see Figure 2.2). UK and EU shipyards are more likely to use non-EVM metrics such as compartment completion (area/zone) and milestones, particularly towards the end of production. Nevertheless, for every phase of production, UK shipyards are more likely than other European shipyards to use earned value metrics as their primary metric for evaluating progress.

Figure 2.2
Percentage of UK, US, and EU Shipbuilders Using Earned Value Metrics

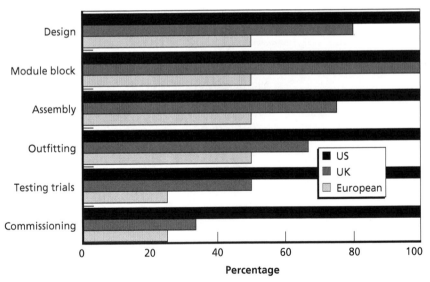

[a] That is, the percentage for firms reporting the use of a metric in a particular phase.
RAND *MG235-2.2*

The US Department of Defense Has Embraced Earned Value Management

The reliance of US shipbuilders on earned value metrics stems from the nation's defence policy requiring the use of EVM on most acquisition programmes of more than $315 million. Contractor programme management systems must conform to the American National Standards Institute standards for EVM. The DoD encourages contractors to use the same system and information for EVM that they use for internal programme control. Contractors report their information at least once a month.

EVM data are reported to the DoD in five formats comprising the Cost Performance Report. The first format reports EVM data by the agreed work breakdown structure (WBS). This reporting is typically limited to no more detail than level 3 of the WBS. The second format reports data by the organisation, such as trade areas (e.g., pipe shop), subcontractor, or other organisations. The third format reviews the programme baseline, any contract changes to the baseline during the reporting period, and the value of management reserve. The fourth format outlines changes in the staffing plan, including workforce trends. The fifth lists problem areas (e.g., those with large variances or poor productivity) and management actions being taken to address them.

How Do Shipbuilders Use Information That Metrics Provide?

Internally, shipbuilders typically use EVM information as a basis of control for internal monitoring of progress. Internal reporting frequency ranged from weekly to more common monthly reports. Internal reports usually have a top-level summary (a window pane or dashboard chart) of the aggregate programme data. These summaries include information on budget cost of work scheduled and performed, actual cost of work performed, and cost performance and schedule performance indices. Shipbuilders also report supporting detail by WBS, organisation, and section or zone of ship.

This information helps the shipbuilder specify areas that are behind or have poor productivity; it is also used to update progress of the network schedules. Representatives of the UK shipyards in particular noted that maintaining and producing a network schedule encompassing more than 10,000 activities in shipbuilding was too difficult to accomplish, especially for defining the *appropriate* logical dependencies among all these activities. However, they said that rolling EVM data progress data into network schedules of approximately 500 activities permitted critical path analysis of overall schedules.

Shipbuilders Employ No Consistent Forecasting Methodology

Shipbuilders differ in how they measure progress and forecast completion. Some rely on critical path analysis, with activity progress determined through EVM. Others, typically cruise-ship builders, use workload analysis to assess likely required and available staffing levels. Some use 'expert judgment', either at the level of foreman and supervisor or at that of project manager, to determine an estimate at completion (EAC). Some use a 'burn rate' method predicting completion based on the rate of task accomplishment during a particular period. Others extrapolate trend lines of cumulative budget costs of work performed.

How Do Other Industries Control Cost and Schedules?

For comparison purposes, we researched means used by a major oil company to measure progress on its projects worldwide, ranging in cost from a few million dollars to a few billion dollars. As part of its control process, this firm demands that contractors have a project team whose members work exclusively on cost and schedule control and that information on progress, cost, and schedule be provided monthly. The information must contain data on actual and planned progress, productivity, the value of equipment and material receipts in the field, and actual-versus-planned staffing. For engineering work, this information must be presented by discipline; for construction activities, it must be provided for both the craft/subcontractor and unit/work area levels. The monthly report must also note major changes and delays, as well as actions to correct any problems, and provide a forecast for the next reporting period. Overall, these information requirements are very similar to those the DoD makes of its contractors.

CHAPTER THREE

What Progress Information Should the DPA Require of Shipbuilders?

The DPA should begin requesting from shipbuilders the basic information needed for earned value management, including core measures on

- actual cost of work performed
- budget cost of work performed
- budget cost of work scheduled
- estimate at completion
- budget at completion.

UK shipbuilders should already have these data readily available because most of them track production progress with EVM. In fact, some shipbuilding programmes, such as that for the Type 45, have already initiated EVM programmes. From these measures, most of the derived earned value metrics can be calculated. Shipbuilders should be asked to provide this information not only at the total programme level but also by WBS, majority activities or tasks, and skills and trades. The DPA and the contractor should agree to the form of detail at the beginning of the programme, but the same approach should not be taken for every contractor. This information should enable the DPA to assess programme progress, identify problem areas, and develop forecasts.

Implementing Earned Value Management

In our discussions with shipbuilders and subsequent literature search, we found several practices that help to create an effective EVM system. Many shipbuilder representatives contended that the lowest level activity actually tracked by an EVM system should be small in work scope, able to be finished within a reporting period. These small tasks have a duration of roughly one week. Tracking small-level tasks in measuring overall progress can help eliminate subjective judgments. Task progress can be assessed using a simple binary measure (done or not done) or through a 50/50 scheme in which a task is considered to be 50 percent complete when it opens and at 100 percent upon completion.

For activities that are difficult to track, such as engineering, fixed guidelines need to be established to assess progress and work scope. One US shipbuilder measures engineering progress based on a 'drawing' having specific design content complete. Progress is assigned when the drawing meets all the criteria for content for one of three levels. Another effective practice is to have major subcontractors report their progress and incorporate these data into overall programme progress reports. For example, BAE Systems incorporates Vosper Thornycroft's progress in reports on the Type 45 programme.

EVM data need to be presented in different ways to be useful. For shipbuilding, this tends to mean presentation by WBS and work centre or trade.

The government (i.e., customer) can also take steps to ensure that an EVM system is effective. The US DoD, for example, limits its data reporting to level 3 of the WBS. Too much data can make analysis, on the government's side, very difficult, since a great amount of data must be manipulated to achieve an overall programme viewpoint. The government should not expect data format to be uniform by contractor but should instead work with data as formatted to reflect the contractor's organisational structure or planning process. Data for evaluating progress should be tied as much as possible to specific tasks or work and not to such elements as level of effort for which there are no specific intermediate products. EVM information should be used to identify problems and develop corrective actions; where used primarily for accounting, it fails to convey all information needed on progress to management. The government may also place representatives on site to ensure it gets the data it needs. The US Navy relies on its Supervisor of Shipbuilding, Repair, and Conversion (or SUPSHIPS) organisation to serve as its on-site monitor of progress and to validate EVM data (although some have argued that such 'micro-supervision' unnecessarily increases overhead costs).

Cost Performance Index

Several studies have focused on the cost performance index (CPI) in DoD programmes.[1] The CPI is the ratio of the budgeted cost to the actual cost of the work performed. The trends and stability of this metric over a programme's life cycle indicate that it is useful in forecasting outcomes (EACs). One study has observed that at between 15 percent and 85 percent of completion, CPI generally does not improve but tends to decline (Beach, 1990). Other research (Christensen and Heise, 1993; Christensen and Payne, 1992) has indicated that once a project is at least 20 percent complete, the cumulative CPI does not vary significantly, and that the variability decreases as the project reaches higher levels of completion. Project forecasts, particularly of the EAC, based on the CPI and the schedule performance index (SPI) tend to be good indicators of final outcomes (Christensen, 1999). EAC based on the CPI and SPI tend to be higher than the contractor's EAC values and are generally more accurate. The CPI can also be used as a check of the contractor's to-complete cost performance index (TCPI), the cost performance assumption for the remaining work, which should be similar to the current cumulative CPI value.

---

[1] See www.suu.edu/faculty/christensend/ev-bib.html (as of July 2004) for an extensive bibliography on EVM articles.

Other Metrics

EVM has some significant limitations for schedule control that must be considered, particularly when using an SPI to evaluate progress (Book, 2003). One of these limitations is that EVM metrics are based directly on cost data (in pounds or worker hours) and have only an indirect link to programme time or duration (although cost and time are generally correlated). EVM assumes a linear correlation between cost and duration for an activity, with tasks or activities weighted by cost. Therefore, an activity that is more costly contributes more to the overall programme SPI than does one that is less costly. Thus, a case of schedule slippage for a low-cost task on the critical path would be masked in the overall SPI for the programme. One advantage of requesting EVM data at the task or activity level is to better understand whether activities on the critical path are slipping.

Because of the limitations of EVM data for schedule management, the DPA should consider some additional progress metrics on shipbuilding programmes. Some shipyard representatives we interviewed said that some installation quantities, such as piping and cable installed, were good monitors of progress, although others noted these metrics were not useful in monitoring progress and were difficult to quantify in practice. During the testing phase, most shipyards use the number of test procedures/plans complete as a metric to assess progress. For commissioning and handover phase of production, many shipyard representatives we interviewed said the number of compartments completed or accepted was a useful metric for measuring progress.

Some other information related to schedule should be tracked. First, the DPA should ask the shipbuilder to provide an updated, forecasted completion date for each progress report. This information should include a revised critical path analysis (based on a high-level schedule described earlier). Such additional information will offset the weaknesses of EVM in weighting by value and ignoring critical path issues. Lastly, the DPA should monitor the value of unresolved (unadjudicated) changes. An estimated value for these changes not in the baseline would help to serve as a check of the EAC and whether the amount of potential new work would make the schedule slip.

Our discussions with shipbuilders and review of relevant literature lead us to recommend that the DPA request EVM data from the shipbuilders to monitor progress. The agency should also track the critical path and completion milestones. Being able to track progress, however, is but one part of the problem the DPA faces in improving schedule adherence. Perhaps a more important issue is to understand the reasons that ships are delivered late and why commercial programmes do much better than military ones. We explore that issue in the next chapter.

CHAPTER FOUR

What Causes Ships to Be Delivered Late, and Why Do Commercial Shipbuilders Have Good Schedule Adherence?

Understanding the reasons underlying schedule delays was a major component of this research. Our survey and interviews of UK, US, and EU shipbuilders included questions regarding the cause of schedule delays. We also sought information on differences in incentives between commercial and military shipbuilding that could contribute to delivering a ship on time.

Change Orders and Late Product Definition: The Leading Contributors to Schedule Slippage

In the survey, we asked each shipbuilder to apportion the factors that contribute to schedule slippage in six general categories. That is, they evaluated the relative contributions of these factors to slippage for their recent programmes such that they added to 100 percent. Figure 4.1 depicts the average value for each category over all the shipbuilders that responded to this question. Of the six categories, the greatest contributor was change orders/late product definition, accounting for nearly half of the reasons shipbuilders cited for being late on projects. The second most cited cause was lack of technical information. We note two clarifications about the figure. First, it represents only the perspective of shipbuilders, not that of clients. Second, the category *change orders/late product definition* does not distinguish whether the client or contractor was responsible for the change; it only notes that a change or definitional issue caused schedule slippage.

Figure 4.1
Causes of Schedule Slips Reported by Shipbuilders (percentage)

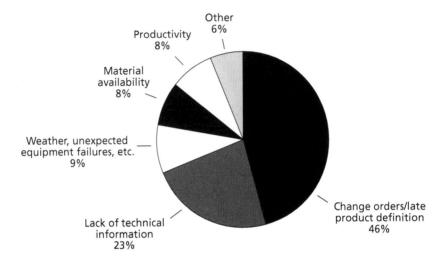

RAND *MG235-4.1*

Commercial Customers Resolve Change Issues Faster and Have Fewer Changes

Shipbuilders told us that they are able to resolve change orders or late definition issues faster with their commercial customers than with their military customers. As we have seen, changes greatly influence delivery time, partly because of the inherent differences in use for military and commercial vessels. Often having the best and most recent equipment and systems, including those developed after design or during construction, can benefit military ships much more than commercial ships. Military ships of a given class may have a unique design, while commercial vessels tend to be more evolutionary or produced from established designs. When changes are made, they are accomplished within just one to four weeks for commercial vessels but require from four to 22 weeks for military ships. Contractors we interviewed also indicated that commercial ship changes, even for complex projects, also tend to be smaller than those for military ships, as indicated by the value of change orders, approximately 4 percent of total vessel cost for new production for commercial ships and approximately 8 percent for military ships.[1]

Thus, one of the aspects of programme management that needs to be considered in any improvement for military production is change management. Commercial customers typically have an on-site representative who can authorise changes. (These representatives may be few in number, helping streamline decisions regarding changes.) For a commercial contract, there is a formal acceptance of the detailed design drawings. Military customers are quite different. The on-site representatives are limited in their authority to make changes; usually changes must be deferred to off-site experts. For UK military ships, there is no formal acceptance of drawings at design. Therefore, inspectors can force significant modifications right up to delivery. Finally, there are multiple stakeholders involved in the procurement of military ships.[2] Therefore, there is no single customer to satisfy; the shipyard must balance competing demands.

Not only do military contracts have more change, but the changes occur much later in the design and build cycle than those for commercial contracts. Most changes on commercial contracts happen during the design phase (see Figure 4.2). By contrast, fewer than 40 percent of the changes on military contracts occur during design. There is a higher proportion of changes on military contracts than on commercial contracts in the later phases of production, particularly at assembly and outfitting. Assembly delays could arise, for example, from poor accuracy control, in which intermediate products are produced on time but assembly is delayed when components do not fit together.

---

[1] Simpler commercial projects tend to require even fewer changes. For example, a $60 million commercial vessel needed about $300,000 in changes. See Buetzow and Koenig (2003).

[2] Stakeholders that have some input include the project team, the fleet, the classification societies, safety groups, inspectors, and so forth.

Figure 4.2
Percentage of Total Number of Changes Occurring at Various
Production Phases

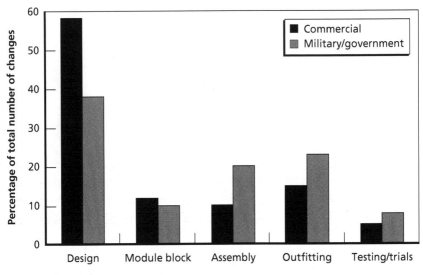

RAND *MG235-4.2*

The consequences of late changes are twofold. First, they are more expensive to implement because already-completed work needs to be redone. In the design phase, only design time is lost through changes. Second, changes lead to additional work that is much more difficult to accomplish in the later stages of construction (e.g., poor access must be overcome).

Commercial Versus Military Payment Incentives

Commercial shipbuilding contract payments and incentives also contribute to on-time delivery. Commercial contracts impose significant liquidated damages, sometimes costing thousands of pounds per day, for late vessel delivery. Such penalties are due to the nature of the business. Commercial customers book passengers or cargo in advance of vessel delivery, meaning late delivery could result in cancellation costs or ill will for the customer. (Military ships, of course, do not face such problems.) Commercial shipbuilders often spend their own money, sometimes through outsourcing some tasks, to avoid liquidated damage penalties and to keep construction on time. Recent DPA shipbuilding programmes, namely Astute and Type 45, do have liquidated damage clauses. These are to cover potential additional costs to the MOD should these programmes slip but are not targeted as schedule incentives. The possibility that such penalties could bankrupt one of the few remaining UK shipbuilders also makes enforcement of such terms problematic. In particular, given the high amount of late change, liability becomes uncertain.

A recent incentive for on-time delivery by commercial builders is their full order books. If one programme has a delay, their other programmes will as well. Because most contracts are fixed-price, commercial shipbuilders want to move production as quickly as possible to maximise profit.

Payment schedules constitute another incentive for commercial builders (see Figure 4.3). Some 80 percent of the contract value is paid on delivery, meaning shipyards carry some of the financial burden, such as construction loan interest payments, of a vessel until the ship is delivered.

By contrast, the DPA pays for military ships by milestones, typically ones that are easily verifiable and evenly spaced over the programme. The milestones are usually negotiated between the DPA and the contractor. The intent is that the payment plan is cash neutral (or slightly negative) with respect to progress (meaning that the shipyard is paid such that its costs for the programme are covered and it does not have to resort to financing as do commercial shipyards). Therefore, the military shipyards do not carry much financial burden for construction.

Some aspects of the DPA Smart Acquisition process allow for a more 'commercial' approach to procurement (MOD, 2004). These approaches include public-private partnership. For example, the Private Finance Initiative transfers financial risk to the private sector. Such approaches permit the DPA, in essence, to contract for a service

Figure 4.3
Percentage of Total Value of Production Payments Paid to
Shipbuilders on Commercial Contracts by Production Phase

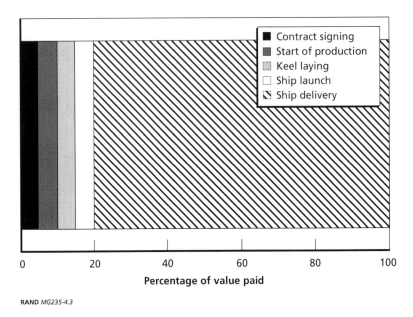

■ Contract signing
▨ Start of production
▨ Keel laying
□ Ship launch
◪ Ship delivery

0   20   40   60   80   100

Percentage of value paid

RAND *MG235-4.3*

and not equipment. Schedule slippage thereby has financial consequences for the firm providing the services. The DPA implemented
this approach with Vosper Thornycroft for the River Class Offshore
Patrol Vessel, but whether such an approach could be used for a warship remains unclear.

Setting Realistic Expectations

Setting appropriate baseline schedules at contract award can help
reduce slippage. The MOD usually sets ship delivery dates based on
operational needs, but it is unclear whether the dates of these forecasted schedules are realistic. If a target is aggressive, the shipyard will
employ riskier strategies, such as overlapping design and construction
or starting construction earlier than an optimal date. The contractor

may not be in a position to say that a schedule is not realistic, particularly for a programme that is competitively bid.

Some programme schedules might be more cost effective from an acquisition standpoint. Shipyards prefer to have stable workload demands. Shifting work might allow more workforce stability, and thereby higher productivity. Shifting start and completion dates for US aircraft carrier programmes helped reduce costs substantially (Birkler et al., 1998). The DPA should work with contractors to better understand the cost sensitivity to schedule.

The DPA should also develop an independent ability to assess programme durations. Shipyards have their own internal 'norms' by which to estimate activity durations. Representatives from the commercial oil firm that we interviewed also described a process they used to forecast programme durations for key phases. The company's independent information is used to validate the contractor schedules and to understand areas of difference. The DPA should be able to develop its own norms based on historical programmes.

As part of the Smart Acquisition process, the DPA has begun to require quantitative risk assessments for cost and schedule. This requirement is know more colloquially as 'three-point estimating'. The goal of these assessments is to define the uncertainty with a schedule or cost estimate by evaluating the minimum, most likely, and maximum outcomes. These data would allow the DPA to better evaluate programme risk. Such approaches generally employ some probabilistic method, such as Monte Carlo analysis (MOD, 2002b). While these approaches are methodologically sound, the results are only as good as the input data. One must be able to evaluate risk distributions for all the components comprising the estimate and to understand the correlations between these elements. Achieving this level of definition is very difficult. If there is bias in the estimates of components (i.e., an estimate is skewed high or low), the quantitative methods will not necessarily reveal the bias and may not provide accurate estimates. We therefore recommend that the DPA devise an independent method to develop schedule norms.

CHAPTER FIVE

Conclusions and Recommendations

Nearly all shipbuilders use earned value management to monitor the progress of production and design. This method is well established in many areas of commercial and military business, not just shipbuilding. As a result, there are extensive training, software, consulting, and literature resources available. Because UK shipbuilders use this methodology as part of their internal control process, the DPA would not, in asking the shipbuilders to develop or implement new systems for tracking EVM metrics, be asking contractors to make extensive innovations for better schedule tracking. In fact, some shipbuilding Integrated Project Teams (IPTs), including that for the Type 45, are already using EVM to control cost and schedule. The DPA could leverage existing investments made by the shipyards if it uses EVM more broadly on shipbuilding programmes. The effective use of EVM, however, will require the DPA to staff IPTs with EVM professionals.

Our analysis of shipbuilding schedule slippage found change orders and late definition to comprise the main cause of delay. There was also a sharp contrast between military and commercial contracts on the level and timing of changes. The level of changes in military shipbuilding contracts were, on average, twice that of commercial contracts. Furthermore, the changes on military contracts occurred much later in the programme cycle. There are some important mission differences for military ships that drive the later changes. Often having the best and most recent equipment and systems can benefit operational effectiveness for military ships. Commercial ships do not need to be as up to date. Furthermore, a given class of military ships tends to be of 'unique' design. In contrast, commercial vessels are likely to be more evolutionary or repeat productions of established designs. Hence, commercial ship designs are generally more mature. Despite the inherent differences in use between military and commercial ships and their implications for change and subsequent schedule slippage indicate, the DPA must take the opportunity to improve its change management on shipbuilding programmes. This action could benefit both cost and schedule performance.

The DPA should consider the following actions to improve the schedule performance of its shipbuilding programmes:

- Develop an internal set of norms, based on prior performance, to gauge whether its plans and contractor proposals are realistic.
- Consider options to control or reduce changes, especially those late in the process, thus minimising programme disruptions and control cost growth.
- Resolve changes quickly. Commercial shipbuilders have representatives on site who are authorised to approve changes; the DPA may consider having a similar individual to manage changes.
- Require shipbuilders to report EVM data that they already track for internal purposes. These data should be provided at least monthly and include updates to the network schedule and critical path analysis.
- Make the EVM process a management control function of the IPT, not simply a cost or accounting function.
- Set appropriate incentives on ship contracts to encourage better schedule performance. As shipbuilding increases in coming years, better schedule performance will be critical to meeting DPA programme expectations and MOD operational needs. Not all incentives used for commercial shipbuilding are appropriate for military shipbuilding, but the DPA could still make schedule incentives a component of any profit or fee structure.

An Overview of Earned Value Management

Project management is a large and well-studied field that comprises several areas, including project time management, cost management, quality management, human resource management, and risk management, among others (Project Management Institute, 2000). One important aspect of the project management process is controlling cost and schedule, which usually relies on some quantitative analysis. The most widely known quantitative method for cost and schedule control is earned value management (EVM). This appendix provides an overview of EVM for those not familiar with it. The key to the success of EVM is that it effectively integrates project cost and schedule to give one measure of project performance.[1] Because cost and schedule are usually highly correlated, this integration is a very attractive feature.

Earned Value

Earned value is basically the value of the work accomplished up to a point in time based on the planned or budgeted value for that work. Project progress is measured against an earnings plan (in dollars or man-hours) and is a variance analysis method that quantifies the deviation of measures of actual performance from a standard. There

---

[1] Project Management Institute (2000). For more information on cost control, see Fisher (1970).

are variations of EVM, such as performance-based EVM—which combines EVM and requirements management by identifying key requirements with the biggest impact on cost, schedule, functionality, technical performance, and risk (Solomon, 2001)—but all share the same underlying methodologies of the earned value concept.

How EVM Is Employed

Computer tools are necessary aids to monitor cost and schedule performance for complex projects. Nevertheless, simple examples suffice to demonstrate EVM.

The process of project schedule and cost control using EVM begins with a work breakdown structure (WBS) disaggregating the work to be performed into small, well-defined tasks. The WBS approach allows planners to estimate more easily the amount of time and cost to complete each activity and to identify dependencies. Resources to perform each task can be identified, and a list of tasks that need to be completed before each task can begin is drawn up. Typically, the tasks are then put into a scheduling programme that produces a sequence of tasks based on project start date, task resource needs, resource availabilities, and task interdependencies. When the tasks in the WBS are put together (or 'rolled up'), the total cost and schedule plan is derived and can be put in spreadsheet or graphical form. These planned costs are referred to as the budgeted cost of work scheduled (BCWS) (Brandon, 1998).

As the project progresses, actual costs are incurred, referred to as actual cost of work performed (ACWP). At each point in time of the project, the budgeted cost of work performed (BCWP) is the expected cost of work up to that point in time.

Table A.1 demonstrates these concepts in simple form. Suppose there is a project to weld 50 pipes. The budgeted cost for the work is $1,000, and it is expected to take 10 days. Therefore, assuming linearity, each pipe has a cost of about $20; the budget is $100 per day; and five pipes have to be welded per day to have 50 by day 10.

Table A.1
Notional Budgeted Cost of Work Schedule

	Day									
	1	2	3	4	5	6	7	8	9	10
Pipes (number)	5	10	15	20	25	30	35	40	45	50
BCWS	$100	$200	$300	$400	$500	$600	$700	$800	$900	$1,000

The manager goes to the work site at day 5 and sees that the project has spent $550 and that 30 pipes have been welded. From Table A.1, it is clear that the BCWS is $500 at day 5, and the BCWP is calculated to be $600 (30 pipes at $20 each). The finance department gives data to the manager saying that $550 has been spent, meaning the ACWP was $550.

Several measures of project progress can be calculated from these data. To determine project deviation from original cost and schedule goals, two measures of variance can be calculated. Cost variance (CV) is the difference between the BCWP and the ACWP, whereas schedule variance (SV) is the difference between the BCWP and the BCWS. In the above example, we calculate the CV (or BCWP − ACWP) as $600 − $550 = $50, which means the value of what the project has accomplished is $50 more than what was spent. A positive CV means that the project is under budget, while a negative CV signifies that the project is over budget. A zero CV indicates that the project is exactly on budget. The SV (or BCWP − BCWS) in the above example equals $600 − $500 = $100, which means the value of what is accomplished to date is $100 greater than the value of what had been planned for that date. A positive SV indicates a project is ahead of schedule; a negative SV signifies it is behind schedule; and a zero SV means it is exactly on time.

Two other measures are used to gauge project progress or completion rates. The schedule performance index (SPI) is equal to BCWP divided by BCWS. In the above example, the SPI is 600 / 500, or 1.2, meaning the project has completed 120 percent of the work originally planned for completion by that date. The cost performance index (CPI) is equal to BCWP divided by ACWP, or 1.09 in the example above, meaning that, for every dollar spent, $1.09 worth of work was performed and that the project is *not* over budget.

An advanced concept of EVM for project monitoring and control is that of the to-complete performance index (TCPI), which is used to monitor the efficiency level that the contractor must achieve in completing the remaining work in order to meet the original budgetary goal. It is computed as a ratio—the quantity of the budget at completion (BAC) minus BCWP (cumulative) divided by the quantity of the BAC minus ACWP (cumulative)—and is interpreted in comparison to the CPI. If the CPI and TCPI are identical, then the project should continue at current level of efficiency to achieve projected budget. If the CPI is less than the TCPI, then efficiency needs to increase to meet budget requirements. If the CPI is greater than the TCPI, then a loss in efficiency could be sustained without affecting project budgetary goals.

The earned value method encompasses many calculations for monitoring and control of project cost and schedule, and it provides many ways of calculating different indices. Appendix B lists a sample of calculations used by EVM practitioners.

EVM Assumptions

There are a number of implicit assumptions underlying EVM. One such notion is that each cost account and its variance are independent, e.g., if the costs of one task go over or under the expected budget, the budgets of other tasks remain unaffected. The assumption of independence of variance is purely mathematical for the purposes of valid computational results. Activities are not, however, always independent.

EVM assumes an inverse linear relationship between activity duration and cost of the resources applied to that activity (Wiest and Levy, 1977). For example, according to this assumption, if 100 men can build a ship in one year, then 200 men could construct the same vessel in six months or 50 men in two years. Most activities can be reduced in duration if extra resources (men, machines, etc.) are provided. This assumption of linearity between time and cost is not always accurate. Furthermore, the productivity of each task is not independent of the performance of other activities.

EVM also assumes that one earned hour is as good as another in terms of progress. In other words, the product of each hour has the same effect on the final product.

EVM Limitations

EVM has a number of limitations. The first is an inability to quickly and effectively implement changes. Computer software programmes that implement these methodologies have relieved some of the burden of manual computational issues, but many other updating problems persist.

Another limitation is data collection and management. Data acquisition required for EVM can be costly and time consuming. Data integrity issues also exist. In many organisations, data on actual costs, even at total project level, cannot be obtained in a timely manner or properly segregated by project. Acquiring an estimate of a particular task's completion requires a deep insight into project workings. Even with very good information, such an estimate may be no more than a guess.

The earned value method lacks flow and value-generation concepts. Flow refers to how resources and activities are sequentially related, whereas value generation denotes allocating a certain weight or value to activities or tasks with respect to their impact on the final product. The lack of flow concepts implies that EVM does not take into consideration supply-chain principles. It also does not permit determination of a critical path or critical activities, as do other schedule planning methods. EVM does not differentiate between value-generating work and non-value-generating work. Value-generating work is work performed now that will allow future work to begin. Non-value-generating work only increases inventories between trades. An example of value-generating work is producing something in a given time period that is required for production in a subsequent period. An example of non-value-generating work is producing spare parts in one period for use in a subsequent period.

Forecasting with EVM

One of the important capabilities of EVM is its ability to forecast final programme cost and schedule. There are many methods to extrapolate EVM to forecast a final cost (Christensen, Antolini, and McKinney, 1995; Christensen, 1993). Most of these cost-forecasting methods project the final cost based on the work accomplished and the work remaining, or estimate to complete (ETC). The ETC is typically based on some measure of efficiency (CPI and SPI) and the budgeted work to complete. The estimate at completion (EAC) refers to the forecasted total programme cost in the EVM vernacular. Forecasts of schedule completion also use some form of extrapolation of an EVM progress metric. The simplest involve the budgeted project duration divided by the SPI.[2]

If the underlying assumptions of EVM are satisfied, particularly that regarding linearity, and if it is possible to get accurate data, then forecasts can be made on expected cost and schedule completion. If the assumptions cannot be satisfied, or the data are inaccurate or were collected improperly, then the estimates will be misleading. Care must also be taken with schedule forecasts such that critical path issues do not dominate the overall schedule prediction.

EVM Extensions

Construction management researchers note a need for a measure of project performance that indicates project maturity or success based on perspective of the customer rather than that of the traditional supplier or contractor. They contend that a measure of success based on

---

[2] For examples of other methods, see Cass (1994) and Lee (2002).

the perspective of the customer will result in more control of workflow and that the value of work from the customer's point of view is based on how much of it can be used. This methodology stems from earned value and is termed customer earned value (CEV) (Kim and Ballard, 2002). This methodology is still being developed, but critical components include some measure of

- quality—with work (counted as CEV) conforming to some quality criteria
- size—with the amount of work being consistent with what the trade contractors and general contractor agreed in preplanning
- pull—with work (counted as CEV) being matched with the products of work that the customer is willing to keep as unused product until those products can be used. For example, part of the project may include the production of spare parts. These spare parts can be produced early and kept in supply until they are needed.

Earned value is equal to customer earned value plus some constant. The difference between EV and CEV is the waste of overproduction, work that does not release downstream work (or work above and beyond that needed to accomplish something else). In shipbuilding, advanced outfitting would mean very little would be performed that does not release work downstream. This methodology and its concepts are still being developed, but they offer promising results for certain applications.

Earned Value Management Calculations

Table B.1, on the following pages, shows common EVM terms along with their definitions and calculations.

Table B.1
EVM Calculations

Term	Definition	Calculation
ACWP (actual cost of work performed)	The costs actually incurred.	
BAC (budget at completion)	The sum of all activity costs established for the project as the baseline budget or an approved revised baseline budget.	
BCWP (budgeted cost of work performed)	The sum of the budgets for completed work packages or tasks and completed portions of open work packages or tasks.	
BCWS (budgeted cost of work scheduled)	The sum of the budgets for the work packages scheduled to be completed at a point in time plus the apportioned budgets for work packages or tasks scheduled to be partially complete at that time.	
CPI (cost performance index)	A measure of the efficiency of the dollar value budgeted for the work performed as a percentage of the dollars spent to do that work. It indicates how many dollars of scheduled effort were accomplished for every dollar spent.	CPI = BCWP / ACWP
CV (cost variance)	A measure of the difference between the cost budgeted for the work performed and the actual cost to do that work.	CV = BCWP − ACWP CV (%) = CV / BCWP
EAC (estimate at completion)	An estimate of the total cost to complete the project at the current performance efficiency.	Example: EAC = BAC / CPI

Table B.1—Continued

Term	Definition	Calculation
ETC (estimate to complete)	An estimate of the remaining cost to complete the project at the current performance efficiency.	*Example:* $ETC = EAC - ACWP$
SPI (schedule performance index)	A measure of the efficiency of performance against the schedule. It indicates how many days of scheduled effort were earned for every day worked.	$SPI = BCWP / BCWS$
SV (schedule variance)	A measure of the difference between the budgeted dollar value of work performed versus the budgeted dollar value of the work scheduled to be completed. Comparing budgeted cost of accomplished work to budgeted cost of scheduled work indicates the difference caused by schedule changes.	$SV = BCWP - BCWS$ $SV\ (\%) = SV / BCWS$
TCPI (BAC) (to-complete performance index within budget amount)	Work remaining divided by money remaining per the original budget estimate. Provides the efficiency improvement required over the budgeted efficiency to finish the project within the baseline budget.	$TCPI\ (BAC) = Work / Money = (BAC - BCWP) / (BAC - ACWP)$
TCPI (EAC) (to-complete performance index within projected estimate to complete)	Work remaining divided by money remaining based on the total estimate at completion, assuming the project efficiency remains unchanged from the current efficiency.	$TCPI\ (EAC) = Work / Money = (BAC - BCWP) / (EAC - ACWP)$

Data Collection Form

On the pages that follow is the data collection form that was sent and completed by the participating shipyards.

Survey on Schedule Control Metrics, Forecasting, and Changes

Introduction

The United Kingdom's Ministry of Defence has asked RAND to conduct a study of scheduling and control practices for shipbuilding.

This survey asks a series of questions about your firm's practices in schedule control and forecasting. We are looking for information that best describes how you currently monitor shipbuilding progress, from design to delivery. We are particularly interested in differences between government and commercial customers, so please highlight any such differences when answering the questions. If there is additional information that might provide a fuller answer to the questions we present below, please attach any relevant documentation to this form.

If you have any questions or require further clarification, please contact one of the RAND analysts listed below.

Thank you for your help.

RAND Contacts
>   John Birkler (310) 393-0411 x7607, birkler@rand.org
>   John Schank (703) 413-1100 x5304, schank@rand.org
>   Mark Arena (703) 413-1100 x5383, Mark_Arena@rand.org

Person(s) Completing the Form

Name	Title	Phone Number	Email Address

Schedule Control and Planning

1. Please describe the general method by which you schedule and monitor work progress. Are the scheduling and control tools employed as support tools (i.e., to measure progress made) or in an executive role (to influence forward planning)?

2. Does the approach change based on the size/value of the work?
   YES _____ NO _____

   If you answered YES, please describe how the approach changes as the size/value of the work changes.

3. Have your scheduling and control techniques changed significantly from previous practice over the past five years?
   YES _____ NO _____

If you answered YES, please describe the change(s), when they occurred, and indicate whether you believe the change(s) resulted in improvements or not.

4. Do you foresee any changes to your scheduling and control techniques to improve the process (e.g., to improve accuracy of forecasting)?
   YES _____ NO _____

   If you answered YES, please identify any constraints that might prevent implementation of these changes.

5. Do you use any programme control/scheduling software?
   YES _____ NO _____

   If you answered YES, please indicate whether you use:
   __ A commercially available progressing and cost-estimating system
      Please identify the system _____
   __ A system that you have procured and modified to meet your needs
      If you use a system that you have procured and modified to meet your needs, please identify the system and explain how you use it.

6. What are the major milestones for which you track progress (completion of design, start of steel fabrication, launch, delivery, and so on)? Is the planning process based on a project/programme life-cycle model? If so, please describe the model.

7. Do you use contract controls/limits to minimize the possibility of delay and disruption?

    YES _____ NO _____

    If you answered YES, which of the following approaches do you use to minimize delay and disruption?

    __ Limiting number of changes customers can request
    __ Limiting kind of changes customers can request
    __ Other (please list)

Metrics

8. In the following matrix [Table 1], please indicate which progress metrics your firm employs to monitor progress. For the primary metric, fill in the box with a 'P'. For a secondary metric(s), fill in the appropriate box(es) with an 'S'. For metrics that are not used, leave the boxes blank. If you employ work subdivisions or measures of progress other than those listed in this table, please fill out an equivalent table using your own divisions and metrics. In doing so, please define the terms you use. If your metrics for government and commercial customers differ, please fill out the table once for each set of customers.

9. Which progress metrics do you routinely report to customers?

    Are the metrics specified by the customer, or do you select them?

Table 1 [from Question 8]

	Design	On-Unit Outfitting	Block Construction	Block Outfitting	Ship Assembly	On-Ship Outfitting	Commissioning/ Testing/Trials
Earned value							
Percentage of estimated cost expended							
Percentage of estimated hours expended							
Schedule performance index (SPI)							
Cost performance index (CPI)							
Work packages							
Available schedule float/contingency							
Milestone/major activity							
Percentage of estimated light ship weight (LSW) installed							
Number of blocks/modules installed							
Number of compartments/ areas accepted by customer							

Table 1 [from Question 8]—Continued

	Design	On-Unit Outfitting	Block Construction	Block Outfitting	Ship Assembly	On-Ship Outfitting	Commissioning/ Testing/Trials
Number of compartments/ areas completed							
Changes not adjudicated							
Percentage of tasks complete by parts count							
Percentage of tasks complete by labour expenditure							
Percentage of tasks meeting originally forecasted start/ completion date							
Other: _____							

Do these metrics effectively convey the schedule progress?

When you report an overall 'percentage complete' metric to the client, how do you determine that value?

10. Do you use different progress metrics for your own use than you report to your customer?
    YES _____ NO_____

    If you answered YES, what metrics do you use, and how do they differ from those you report to your customers?

11. Do you use parametric estimating relationships for developing project cost and schedule estimates?
    YES _____ NO _____

    If you answered YES, are these relationships based on only in-house data?
    YES _____ NO _____

    Are they updated for recent projects?
    YES _____ NO _____

    Are they based on return costs?
    YES _____ NO _____

    What are the units (pounds/dollars per weight of ship or system, pounds/dollars per unit of work, etc.) of the costs and schedule estimates from the parametric relationships?

Forecasting

12. How do you forecast completion dates using the metrics above?

13. Are certain metrics better than others for forecasting end-of-job date?
    YES _____ NO _____

    If you answered YES, please list those metrics that are best for forecasting the end of a job.

14. Are your cost and schedule estimates updated during the course of a project?
    YES _____ NO _____

    If you answered YES, how frequently are they updated and how are the updates used?

Results

16. If possible, please provide an example of your primary progress metric(s) plotted versus time for a recently completed ship.

17. What is the average difference between the forecast delivery date at contract and the actual date?

    How does the difference between the forecast delivery date at contract and the actual date vary from ship to ship (i.e., is the difference fairly consistent from ship to ship, or does it vary for each ship)?

18. What are the most common reasons for errors in the forecast completion date?

19. Do your ship contracts typically have a schedule incentive/penalty clause?
    YES _____ NO _____
    If you answered YES, please describe the clause.

20. How would you apportion the source of delays and cost increases above original estimates for recent projects? Please fill out the table below [Table 2] and add any other categories you think appropriate.

Change

21. How are scope changes and change orders addressed with respect to the schedule plan/control for a *government customer*?

    For a *commercial customer*?

22. For *government customers*, please indicate [in Table 3] the percentage of changes that occur during each phase of construction.

For *commercial* customers, please indicate [in Table 4] the percentage of changes that occur during each phase of construction.

24. Of the total programme value for a typical *government* project, what percentage is attributable to changes?

Of the total programme value for a typical *commercial* project, what percentage is attributable to changes?

25. What is the typical length of time (in weeks) it takes to adjudicate a change for a *government* customer? For a *commercial* customer?

Table 2 [from Question 20]

	Customer Changes or Late Product Definition	Inability to Obtain Material on Time	Inability to Obtain Technical Information on Time	Lower Labour Productivity Than Anticipated	Weather, Unexpected Equipment Failure, Acts of God	Other
Percentage of total delay						
Percentage of total cost increase						

Table 3 [from Question 22a]

	Design	Unit Outfitting	Block Construction	Block Outfitting	Ship Assembly	In/On-Ship Outfitting	Testing/Trials
Percentage of total number of changes							

Table 4 [from Question 22b]

	Design	Unit Outfitting	Block Construction	Block Outfitting	Ship Assembly	In/On-Ship Outfitting	Testing/Trials
Percentage of total number of changes							

References

Beach, Chester Paul, Jr, 'A-12 Administrative Inquiry,' Memorandum for the Secretary of the Navy, 28 November 1990.

Birkler, John, Michael Mattock, John Schank, Giles Smith, Fred Timson, James Chiesa, Bruce Woodyard, Malcolm MacKinnon, and Denis Rushworth, *The U.S. Aircraft Carrier Industrial Base: Force Structure, Cost, Schedule, and Technology Issues for CVN 77*, Santa Monica, Calif., USA: RAND Corporation, MR-948-NAVY/OSD, 1998. Online at www.rand.org/publications/MR/MR948/ (last accessed July 2004).

Book, S., 'Point Counter Point: Revisiting "What Is the Health of My Project—the Use and Benefit of Earned Value",' *National Estimator*, Fall 2003, pp. 11–15.

Brandon, Daniel M., 'Implementing Earned Value Easily and Effectively', *Project Management Journal*, Vol. 29, No. 2, June 1998, pp. 11–18.

Buetzow, Mark R., and Philip C. Koenig, 'Mission and Owner's Requirements', in Thomas Lamb, ed., *Ship Design and Construction*, Jersey City, N.J., USA: Society of Naval Architects and Marine Engineers, 2003, pp. 7-1 to 7-23.

Cass, Donald J., 'Improve Schedule Forecasting Via Earned Value', *AACE Transactions*, 1994, pp. CSC7.1–9.

Christensen, David S., 'The Estimate at Completion Problem: A Review of Three Studies', *Project Management Journal*, Vol. 24, 1993, pp. 37–42.

_____, 'Using Earned Value Cost Management Report to Evaluate the Contractor's Estimate at Completion', *Acquisition Quarterly Review*, Vol. 19, Summer 1999, pp. 283–296.

Christensen, David S., Richard Antolini, and John W. McKinney, 'A Review of Estimate at Completion Research', *Journal of Cost Analysis and Management*, Spring 1995, pp. 41–62.

Christensen, David S., and Scott R. Heise, 'Cost Performance Index Stability', *National Contract Management Journal*, Vol. 25, 1993, pp. 7–15.

Christensen, David S., and Kirk S. Payne, 'CPI Stability: Fact or Fiction?' *Journal of Parametrics*, Vol. 10, April 1992, pp. 27–40.

Fisher, Gene H., *Cost Considerations in Systems Analysis*, Santa Monica, Calif., USA: RAND Corporation, R-0490-ASD, 1970.

Kim, Yong-Woo, and Glenn Ballard, 'Earned Value Method and Customer Earned Value', *Journal of Construction Research*, Vol. 3, No. 1, March 2002, pp. 55–66.

Lee, David, 'Norden-Raleigh Analysis: A Useful Tool for EVM in Development Projects', *The Measurable News*, March 2002, pp. 21–24.

MOD—*see* UK Ministry of Defence.

NAO—*see* UK National Audit Office.

PA News, 'Former BAE Chief Reveals Bidding Secrets', *Times Online*, 23 January 2004. Online at http://business.timesonline.co.uk/article/ 0,,8209-974580,00.html (as of July 2004).

Project Management Institute, *A Guide to the Project Management Body of Knowledge*, Newtown Square, Pa., USA, 2000.

Scott, Richard, 'Delays Hit UK Landing Ship Programme', *Jane's Defence Weekly*, 14 January 2004.

Solomon, Paul, 'Practical Software Measurement, Performance-Based Earned Value', *Crosstalk*, September 2001.

UK Ministry of Defence, *Performance Report 2001/2002*, November 2002a. Online at www.official-documents.co.uk/document/cm56/5661/ contents.htm (last accessed July 2004).

_____, *Quantitative Risk Analysis Process Guide for Risk Practitioners*, December 2002b.

_____, *Annual Report and Accounts 2002/2003*, October 2003. Online at www.mod.uk/publications/performance2002/index.htm (as of July 2004).

_____, *The Smart Acquisition Handbook: A Guide to Achieving 'Faster, Cheaper, Better and More Effectively Integrated'*, 5th edition, January 2004. Online at www.ams.mod.uk/ams/content/handbook/front.htm (as of July 2004).

UK National Audit Office, *Ministry of Defence: Major Project Reports 2002*, December 2002. Online at www.nao.org.uk/publications/nao_reports/ 02-03/020391.pdf (as of July 2004).

Wiest, Jerome D., and Ferdinand K. Levy, *A Management Guide to PERT/CPM*, Englewood Cliffs, N.J., USA: Prentice-Hall, 1977.